SUPER-CHARGED!

MOTOCROSS CYCLES

BY

Paul Estrem

EDITED BY

Howard Schroeder, Ph.D.
Professor in Reading and Language Arts
Dept. of Curriculum and Instruction
Mankato State University

CRESTWOOD HOUSE
New York

CIP

LIBRARY OF CONGRESS CATALOGING IN PUBLICATION DATA

Estrem, Paul.
  Motocross cycles.

  (Super-charged!)
  Includes index.
  SUMMARY: Introduces the sport of motocross motorcycles, their distinctive features, clothing for riding, and safety tips for riding dirt bikes.
  1. Motorcycles, racing—Juvenile literature. 2. Motocross—Juvenile literature. [1. Motorcycles. 2. Motocross] I. Schroeder, Howard. II. Title.
TL440.E88   1987   629.2'275—dc19   87-16115
ISBN 0-89686-354-9

International Standard Book Number: 0-89686-354-9	Library of Congress Catalog Card Number: 87-16115

CREDITS

Illustrations:
Cover Photo: J. Madeley/Hillstrom Stock Photo
Tony M. Powers: 5, 7, 10, 13, 14, 17, 18-19, 21, 22, 24-25, 28-29, 30, 33, 34-35, 40-41, 44
Thom Veety/Action Photos: 8, 27, 37, 39, 43
Graphic Design & Production:
Baker Street Productions, Ltd.
Technical Assistance:
Steven Jacobsen

Copyright © 1987 by Crestwood House, Macmillan Publishing Company

Macmillan Publishing Company
866 Third Avenue
New York, NY 10022
Collier Macmillan Canada, Inc.

CRESTWOOD HOUSE

Printed in the United States of America
First Edition
10   9   8   7   6   5   4

TABLE OF CONTENTS

INTRODUCTION

Jason woke up suddenly when the bus began to slow down. The soft light shining through the windows told him that it was morning. He looked at his little brother, Davy, curled up on the seat next to him. Davy was sleeping soundly. As the bus rolled into the station, Jason saw a sign that said "River Bend." They'd arrived!

"Davy, Davy, wake up," Jason whispered as he gently shook his brother's shoulder. "We're here—we're at Matt's and Paige's!" Jason saw his two cousins on the platform waving and smiling at the bus. Uncle Dan and Aunt Nancy were standing behind them.

"All out for River Bend," the driver called. Jason and Davy hurried down the aisle to the front of the bus. The bright morning sun greeted them as they hopped down the steps and out the door.

"Welcome!" cousin Matt shouted as Jason and Davy ran toward their relatives. Both Jason and Matt were twelve years old, but Jason saw at once that Matt had outgrown him by a few inches during the past year.

Aunt Nancy and Paige laughed as they hugged the two travelers. "Good to have you back in River Bend, boys," Uncle Dan said as he shook their hands. "We've got a lot to show you since you were here last year!"

Uncle Dan quickly got the boys' bags from the bus driver and loaded them into the back of the open-top

Action is never far away when you've got an MX cycle!

Jeep. "I suppose you boys are expert freestylers on your bikes now, huh?" Matt asked as they drove toward the ranch. "I quit riding my BMX a few months ago. Dad convinced me that horsepower works better out on the ranch," he said, smiling.

"You're still riding that horse your dad gave you?" Jason asked. "Nope," Matt replied, "Dad went through the stable and found a better one. You'll see when we get there."

At the ranch, Jason and Davy got settled in the guest bedroom. After they called their parents to tell them that they'd arrived safely, everyone sat down to breakfast at the backyard picnic table.

"Matt told us that you got him a new horse, Uncle Dan," Jason said as he finished a tall glass of orange juice. Matt quickly added, "Horsepower, Dad, horsepower!" Uncle Dan looked at Matt, smiled, and replied, "I think Matt's got some explaining to do, boys. You'd better show them the horsepower you're talking about, Matt."

"OK, Dad," Matt said as he stood up. He pushed his chair back and started to walk toward the barn. "Horsepower, you guys, horsepower," he said as he went into the stable. Jason and Davy glanced at each other, puzzled.

A few moments later, a strange, mechanical sound could be heard inside the barn. Suddenly, the cracking sound of a small unmuffled engine filled the barn. Jason and Davy looked at each other in surprise.

The engine revved again, followed by the clunk of shifting gears. The next thing the boys saw was Matt, racing out of the barn on a bright red motocross dirt bike. He circled once and did a quick wheelie. Then he drove up to the boys and shut the engine off. "So that's the 'horsepower' you've been talking about!" Jason exclaimed.

"Yup," Matt replied with a big grin. "And I've been wondering how long a BMX freestyler like you can stay on it without getting thrown. We'll find out when we take her out to the hills this morning. Your BMX bike just won't feel the same when you get home, Jay!"

If you're an experienced MX rider or racing fan, you already know why Matt was so excited about sharing his motocross dirt bike with his cousin from the city. If you're new to motocross, you probably have the same questions about MX cycles that Jason must have had.

A motocross racer does a quick wheelie.

WHY THEY'RE CALLED "MX" MOTORCYCLES

The first motorcycle was invented almost one hundred years ago. It was nothing more than a bicycle with a motor attached to it. The words ''motor'' and ''bicycle'' were combined to make the word ''motorcycle.''

Until the late 1930's, the most popular motorcycles were large, heavy machines. They were designed to be driven mostly on roads. When riders became more

By the early 1960's, people all over the country were excited about MX racing. Today, it's as popular as ever.

interested in off-the-road motorcycle racing, they started to look for smaller, lighter and faster machines. Many of them modified their own motorcycles to do better during races.

By the 1940's, American motorcycle companies had started to design and build machines that were easier to handle off the road. Lightweight frames and smaller tires made these new machines easy to drive through mud, loose sand and gravel.

In the late 1950's, several motorcycle companies from foreign countries began to sell motocross bikes in the United States. The most popular dirt-bike manufacturers at that time still dominate the market today: Honda, Kawasaki, Suzuki and Yamaha. Other well-known MX bike companies include Bultaco, Husqvarna, Maico and Montessa.

Cross-country motorcycle racing with these faster, lighter machines soon became popular. As the sport became organized and more widespread, it was officially named "motocross" by combining the words "motorcycle" and "cross country." The abbreviation for "motocross" is "MX."

Like many fads, motocross racing first became popular on the West Coast. By the early 1960's, MX racing had become a very popular spectator sport throughout the nation. Thousands of motocross fans went to the tracks each weekend to see their favorite dirt bikes in action.

CAN ANYONE RIDE AN MX DIRT BIKE?

A driver's license or special training is not legally required to ride an MX motorcycle. (Special training and supervision for MX beginners is always recommended, though.) There aren't any age restrictions for MX riders, either. In fact, official motocross races have been sponsored for riders as young as six years old.

Motorcycle manufacturers build MX cycles in many different sizes. It doesn't matter if you're young, old, small or large. You will certainly be able to find an MX cycle sized just right for you and with the right amount of power.

MX bikes and riders come in all sizes.

10

WHERE CAN YOU RIDE AN MX CYCLE?

Motocross motorcycles are "off-the-road" dirt bikes. They are <u>not</u> built for riding on streets, roads or highways. In fact, it is illegal and unsafe to drive an MX dirt bike on any public road. Standard MX bikes are not equipped with the turn signals, rearview mirrors and other road safety features required by law for on-road vehicles.

MX bikes must be driven only on private property. If you live in the country, it will probably be easy for you to find good places to ride. If you live in a city, you will have to find an MX track or other private property on which to ride.

ARE MOTOCROSS MOTORCYCLES FOR EVERYONE?

Not everyone has the chance to compete with MX motorcycles. But MX riding and racing are almost as exciting for those watching as for the riders themselves. Every weekend, thousands of MX fans flock to motocross tracks across the country for high-speed thrills that are hard to match! If there's no MX track close to where you live, a wide variety of MX magazines and newsletters are available at most motorcycle stores.

Many MX riders like to use their dirt bikes just for slow, reliable transportation on rough terrain. Being able to ride through wild, scenic areas has given many MX riders a freedom they never had before. Sidecars are often used on MX bikes, so that more than one rider can enjoy the ride and the scenery.

HOW MX DIRT BIKES ARE DIFFERENT FROM OTHER MOTORCYCLES

We've already mentioned a few of the differences between MX "dirt bikes" and other types of motorcycles. Generally, MX bikes are smaller, lighter and easier to handle on rough terrain. But there are other differences as well. The following pages will help you better understand these differences.

Handlebars

Most "street" motorcycles are equipped with a set of high-rise handlebars that sweep to the rear and downward. The instruments, turn signals and rearview mirrors are mounted on the bars. MX handlebars, on the other hand, are built rugged to withstand spills and slides. Most of them are bent back only slightly and are reinforced with a cross brace and protective pad. Turn signals and mirrors are never used. The only

On rough terrain, MX bikes are easier to handle than other types of motorcycles.

instrument used on most MX bikes is a trip meter to record mileage.

Tires

Standard motorcycles most often use tires with smooth treads to hug the pavement. Motocross bikes are always equipped with knobby tires to give the best traction on rough terrain. The rear tire is usually a bit smaller, but wider, to provide the best gripping power. The front tire is bigger in diameter, but narrower, to

13

An MX front fork must stand up to bumpy ground and hard jumps.

give the best steering control. Since several MX bike sizes are available, tire sizes vary.

Wheel Rims

Both front and rear-wheel rims take a beating during an MX race. There's a lot of jumping, turning and hard landings. For this reason, MX wheel rims are built more rugged than the rims on a street motorcycle. Rims are usually built of reinforced aluminum alloy, which is both lightweight and strong.

Front Fork

The front forks on most street motorcycles are made to take mild bumps at the most. Rider comfort is the main concern. MX dirt-bike front forks, in contrast, are designed to take a constant beating. The front forks on some bikes come with air-assisted shock absorbers that will move up to 9 inches (23 cm) after an especially hard landing.

Frame

MX motorcycle frames are built very strong to take heavy stress. Extra braces add support. A typical MX frame is built small and mounted high to allow the greatest amount of clearance from the ground. This way, the frame won't "bottom out" after a very hard landing. The bike will also be able to travel over large rocks and other objects without getting "hung up." A special engine guard on the bottom of the frame protects the engine from damage on rough ground.

Saddle

Most MX riding is done standing up, sitting straight

or crouched down low. The rider often must slide back as far as possible to provide the most traction on the rear wheel, which is where the power comes from. The most popular MX saddle is a long bench seat mounted low on the frame. The seat is out of the way when the driver is standing up. It is also low enough to provide instant foot action on the ground when the driver is sitting down.

Engine

Street motorcycles are available with many different engine sizes, but they are usually bigger and heavier than motocross engines. Motocross engines are often selected according to the size and weight of each rider. The smallest engine used is the 60cc (cubic centimeters). This is often used on MX cycles for children as young as six years old. A popular mid-range engine size is 125cc, which provides more than enough power for an average teenager. Heavy competition bikes, driven by adult professionals, often use engines as large as 600cc. MX engines are built mostly from lightweight aluminum.

Gear Box

MX cycles are usually made with five or six gears to provide the most power or speed during a race. Gears are usually shifted by tapping or lifting a short throw lever with the left foot.

Brakes

The front-wheel brake on an MX cycle is worked

by a lever on the right-hand handlebar grip. The rear brake is controlled by pressing a foot lever with the right foot.

Fenders

Most standard street cycles come with close-fitting fenders on both wheels. MX cycles also have fenders to protect the driver from flying water, mud, gravel and rocks. The difference is that MX fenders are mounted high above each wheel. This allows the rugged suspension systems on each wheel to collapse and expand after a bump or hard landing.

Notice the bench seat and lightweight engine on this racer.

Chainguard

Chainguards are most often used on street cycles to protect both the rider and the chain. MX cycles seldom have chainguards, since the rider usually wears heavy boots. Also, most riders want to reach the chain quickly if it breaks or falls off.

Protective Pads & Shielding

MX cycle handlebars sometimes have shock pads

Like most MX bikes, this one has lightweight disc brakes—but no chainguards.

mounted on them. Gas tanks are set low so they will not be a safety hazard. Rear-fender side guards and exhaust-system covers are also used to protect the rider's legs and feet. Helmets, goggles, padded garments, gloves and other protective wear should always be worn when riding.

GETTING READY TO RIDE—THE MX BASICS

Whether you're new to MX cycle riding or a pro, you will enjoy riding most if you remember some riding and safety "basics." This is true for organized racing, riding around in the hills on a Saturday afternoon, or putt-putting quietly down a forest trail.

Your MX cycle is built to take a lot of punishment. But it has weaknesses, too. It's important to know what those weaknesses are. The MX "basics" are important for another reason. You should understand them in order to protect yourself—and others—no matter where you're riding. Before you ride your cycle, you should always think about the following MX basics.

Clothing

Always wear suitable clothes when you ride your cycle. This is important for both comfort and safety. The trick is to think about what you're going to do on your cycle before you go.

Are you going out to run a quick errand? Your regular school clothes and a jacket will be fine in good weather. But you will have to remember not to try anything fancy! Are you going to spend the morning exploring a wild off-the-road area with some friends? It would be smart to wear your most rugged protective gear. You will most likely take a few spills.

20

Wearing proper clothes and safety gear is very important!

Boots are the best choice of footwear for MX racing or hill climbing.

Remembering to keep all parts of your body well covered while riding is best for your safety. If you take a spill, you will have a better chance of not getting cuts and bruises. Shirts and jackets should be loose enough to give your arms freedom of movement. Trousers or riding pants should be tight in the legs so they won't get caught in the drivetrain.

What about shoes and socks? For most day-to-day casual riding, your favorite tennis shoes will be fine. For heavy racing or hill climbing, boots are the best choice. If you're wearing shoes, make sure they're the kind with laces—and that they're tied securely. You won't want them to fall off during a tricky move!

Special MX Protective Gear

Selecting the right riding clothes is important. Using special MX protective gear is even more important. MX cycling is a power-packed, rough-and-tumble sport. The best way to be prepared for a spill is to use proper gear at all times.

Head and face injuries can be the most serious. A good helmet and goggles are essential! Always wear your helmet, even on short, quiet trips.

Official competitions require that you wear special MX gloves, protective pads, boots and garments. You should always wear them during practice, too.

You can find special MX riding pants, shirts, jackets, and one-piece suits at most cycle shops. They are light-weight, rugged and provide a lot of comfort and protection. Most of them have built-in protective pads.

Frequent safety checks will help keep your machine in top condition—so you can do stunts like this!

Safety Check!

Before riding, you should always check over your MX bike. You can avoid many problems by using the simple ten-point checklist below. And remember, if you don't know how to adjust or fix a part, don't try to do it yourself!

1. Check handlebars for position and tightness. Check all protective gear.
2. Check front and rear brakes.
3. Check frame, front fork and rear suspension.
4. Check wheel alignment and tightness.
5. Check spoke condition and tire pressure.
6. Check condition and tightness of chain sprockets.
7. Check chain condition and tension.
8. Check engine and ignition system.
9. Check fuel supply.
10. Check all bolts and fasteners for tightness.

And don't forget: If you're going to park your cycle, be sure that you have a strong motorcycle chain and lock!

Off-The-Road MX Rules

Whether you're racing, climbing hills or just riding in a park, you should always keep the following set of MX riding rules in mind:

• Ask your local police department about MX cycle rules and always obey them.

• Never "ride" or "buck" a passenger on your cycle. Your MX cycle was made to carry one passenger—you!

Always keep both hands on the handlebars.

- When driving in a park, always yield to other vehicles and be polite to pedestrians. Use hand signals for stops and turns.
- Always use extra caution at night or in bad weather.
- Always keep both hands on the handlebars.

Racing on a dirt track is one of the most exciting MX challenges.

THE ONE THAT STARTED IT ALL: MOTOCROSS DIRT TRACK!

There's nothing quite like a howling pack of MX racers in a "dirt track" competition. The key to all the excitement, of course, is the MX dirt track itself. If we used only one word to describe an MX dirt track, it

would have to be "hazards."

Looking out over a dirt track is like looking at an outdoor construction site. The entire area is filled with hills, water holes, mud pits, large and small bumps, and loose sand and gravel. When six or eight MX cycles and their riders are added to the scene, it becomes a thrilling place!

Tabletop jumps add to the fun by sending riders across a flat surface—and then over a sharp drop at the far end. Bikes and riders often end up in a heap at the bottom of these jumps. High jumps shoot cyclers up and over a tall peak. Water and mud jumps often produce messy results! And when riders hit ''bunny hops'' or ''whoop-de-do's'' too fast, there's not much they can do but try to pick the best spot to fall.

''Berms'' are fast turns banked to the inside, and good drivers know how to use them to get the most speed. Flat turns, on the other hand, are not banked. It's easy to slide out if you're going too fast. The final stretch before the finish line is usually flat, giving slower racers a final chance to catch up. There's always a winner!

Bumps and jumps add to the thrill of MX racing.

STRAIGHT UP:
MX HILL CLIMBING!

Often called "ride-or-slide," MX motorcycle hill climbing can be just as spectacular to watch as MX dirt-track racing. The big challenge, however, is not a series of hazards. There's only one hazard: a big, steep hill. For the same reasons that some of the best downhill skiers won't go off a ski jump, many dirt-track riders won't take on a long, steep hill!

The goal of hill climbing, of course, is to get to the top. This sounds easy, especially if you're not being timed. The truth is that many riders never make it to the top.

An MX hill climb usually starts out in an orderly fashion at the bottom of the hill. When the starting gun goes off, all the bikes and riders appear to be headed in the same direction: up. Within seconds, however, the hillside begins to look like a hive swarming with bees—all going in different directions.

Soon, many riders are separated from their bikes by making one of two mistakes. First, they may spin their rear wheel too fast and end up laying the bike on its side. Second, hill climbers often let a "wheelie" get out of control. A wheelie on a steep hill can quickly flip an MX bike right over on its back. What goes up must come down!

How do the riders keep their loose bikes from running

away from them down the hill? Each hill-climbing bike is equipped with a special "kill switch." This device shuts the engine off instantly. A cord is connected from the kill switch to the rider's wrist before the race. If the rider loses his bike, the wrist cord will yank the switch and shut the bike's engine off.

The secret of successful hill climbing is to keep the cycle moving toward the top of the hill without spinning the rear wheel or letting the front wheel get up off the ground. Speed, control, an excellent sense of balance—and nerves of steel—are needed to get the winning hill climber to the top.

THE LONG HAUL: ENDURO RACING!

Motocross "enduro" racing got its start in the sandy, hot desert areas of the West Coast. "Survival of the fittest" is the key to winning these endurance races. In fact, enduro racing tests the fitness of the rider as much as the motorcycle. Both bike and rider have to be in top shape to stick with these races to the end—and win.

Besides being a talented rider, each MX enduro rider must also be skilled in map reading, desert survival skills and motorcycle maintenance. If an enduro bike breaks down, the rider is the only one around to fix it!

A hill climber keeps his weight forward to prevent a wheelie.

An MX rider takes to the air.

MX enduro riders usually take off in different directions at the beginning of a long race. Each rider hopes that the route he has selected is the best one. In long-haul enduro races, riders often will not see another person for several days. It's just the rider and his sturdy bike against the intense desert heat.

THE MX BALANCING ACT: SLOW-BUT-STEADY TRIALS!

MX "trials" riders pay more attention to balance than speed. First, they pick out a very difficult course over rough terrain. Then, one by one, they try to make it through the course without touching their feet to the ground. Each time a foot touches the ground to balance the bike, the rider loses a point.

Some of the best MX trials riders have even learned how to go backwards during a "trial" run!

As more and more people become involved in MX riding, they'll probably come up with even more ways to compete on MX cycles. The fun and excitement of the MX world will go on!

Whether they chose racing, hill climbing, enduro racing or trials, MX riders are always facing exciting challenges.

AN MX MORNING

Cousin Matt and his two friends, Mike and John, each had made several noisy runs up the side of a steep, grassy hill on their dirt bikes. The chrome pieces on the bikes shone in the sunlight as they danced and zigzagged up the hill. Jason, Davy, Paige, Aunt Nancy and Uncle Dan watched them from under a large shade tree at the foot of the hill.

"This is the only hill we allowed Matt to practice on when he first got his bike," Uncle Dan said. "The dirt trail is narrow and there's tall, thick grass all the way up the hill. Just like falling on a mattress."

"I don't think I'd like to try that, Uncle Dan," Davy said. Aunt Nancy laughed and replied, "You don't have to, Davy. In fact, we told your mom and dad that you're not big enough yet to ride a dirt bike the same size as Matt's. We'll just watch for now."

Uncle Dan turned and smiled at Jason. "How about you, Jay? Matt's been talking about getting you on that machine ever since he got it." Uncle Dan waved his arms at the three riders as they began to bounce and swerve back down the hill, their engines idling. Matt, Mike and John pulled up and stopped by the others under the shade tree. Mike and John shut their engines off.

"Ready for a spin, Jay?" Matt asked as he pulled his helmet off. His engine was still idling. "I've been telling Mike and John about your fancy BMX freestyling. Maybe you could show us some city tricks on this!" The three riders smiled at each other. Without wasting a moment, Jason replied, "You bet, Matt. Promise you won't laugh if it gets away from me?"

Wipeouts do happen—even to experienced riders.

Stunts like this take a lot of practice.

"Not really," Matt chuckled. "Remember how you laughed when I tried those BMX freestyle tricks you showed me last year? Here, put my helmet on and get ready for a real ride." Jason grinned at Matt as he strapped the helmet on. He also put on Matt's thick leather jacket and riding gloves. "I've never done this before, Matt!" Jason said, his voice muffled behind the face guard. "I'm sure it's simple, though," he said.

Matt held the bike steady as Jason climbed on. Uncle Dan then told Jason how to use the brakes, clutch and gearshift. "Ready to rip, Jason?" Matt asked. Jason nodded and gripped the handlebars tight. Matt and Uncle Dan let go of the bike and stepped back. Jason waved at the small crowd as he revved the engine a few times. He pulled in the clutch handle, applied the brakes to both wheels and kicked the gearshift lever into first gear. He then pointed the front wheel at the trail leading up the hill.

Everyone moved back as Jason raced the engine and let go of the clutch lever. The rear wheel spun in the dirt, but the bike didn't take off the way it should have. The wildly spinning rear wheel slipped out from under Jason and spun the bike off into the grass. Jason was left sitting in the dirt where the bike should have been. He had forgotten to let go of the front brake!

Matt quickly ran to his bike and shut the engine off. Everyone started to laugh when they saw that Jason was a bit dusty but unhurt. "That was quite a freestyle trick

Riding an MX cycle isn't always as easy as it looks.

on your first run, Jay," Matt said as he helped Jason up off the ground.

Jason took off Matt's helmet and grinned sheepishly as he brushed the dirt off his clothes. "Maybe I'll just watch you guys for a while," Jason said. "I think you country folks understand this kind of horsepower better than city folks!"

The exciting world of MX has plenty to offer everyone.

IS ORGANIZED MX RIDING FOR YOU?

Like Jason, maybe you're just getting your first taste of MX riding. Or maybe you've been riding for a while but have never seen or taken part in an official MX competition. How can you learn more?

The quickest way to learn more is to visit an MX track or event in your area. You will be able to meet lots of people who love MX cycling and know a lot about it. They will be happy to tell you how to get involved.

Another way is to talk to your nearest MX motorcycle dealer. They will be glad to tell you about MX groups and events in your area. They can also tell you how to get MX newsletters and magazines. This way, you can contact national MX organizations and keep up with the latest developments in MX activities.

Whether you want to race at a dirt track, climb hills, or just drive peacefully through a forest, the world of MX has a lot to offer you!

GLOSSARY / INDEX

ACCESSORIES 19, 23 — *Extra or special equipment, such as helmets, gloves, and riding boots.*

ALLOY 15 — *Two or more metals mixed together.*

BERM 30 — *A fast turn banked to the inside.*

BRAKES 16

BUNNY HOP 30 — *Series of low bumps on a track.*

CHAINGUARD 18

CLOTHING 19, 20, 23

DIRT BIKE 9, 11, 12, 28 — *MX bike equipped specifically for MX motocross racing.*

ENDURO 32, 36 — *Long-distance endurance racing on MX motorcycles.*

ENGINE 16

FENDERS 17

FRAME 15

FRONT FORK 15

GEAR BOX 16

HANDLEBARS 12, 17

KILL SWITCH 32 — *A special switch on an MX hill-climbing bike that shuts the motor off instantly if the driver falls off.*

MOTOCROSS 9, 11 — *Cross-country motorcycle racing.*

MX 7, 9, 10, 11, 12, 15, 20, 26, 28, 31, 36, 45 — *Abbreviation for "motorcycle motocross."*